IN LOVING MEMORY OF

IN REMEMBRANCE OF
Corey Schmitt
1987-2022

Bastion Porter Cohen
Our sweet baby Bash
2020

Carol Bradley
"Granny"
1943-2019

Christmas isn't the same without you, xox

Library of Congress Control Number 2023917526
Publication Cataloging-in-Publication Data
ISBN Hardcover 979-8-9872987-4-9
ISBN Paperback 979-8-9872987-3-2
ISBN ebook 979-8-9872987-5-6

Printed in the United States of America

Publishing Services provided by Rebel Queen
https://rebelqueen.co/
Social media: @rebelqueenbooks

Eden and Ellie's
Christmas is Not the Same

For families coping with grief and loss during the holiday season

By: Autumn & Brandon Cohen

Illustrated By: Bridget Wallace

Grab your coat.
Winter is here.

A season of joy.

BUT NOT THIS YEAR.

"It's Christmas time," friends chant and cheer! I can't help but notice, we're not all here.

My friends don't know someone special has died.

IT'S AWFUL!
THE WORST.

C'mon Ellie, let's go back inside.

This home has felt sad.
It's just not the same.
My eyes get all teary
when I hear their name.

Still, this is Christmas.
A festive holiday.
Out come the boxes.
Ellie, this is no time to play.

Ornaments, wreaths, and flashing lights,
old Christmas traditions will never
feel quite right.

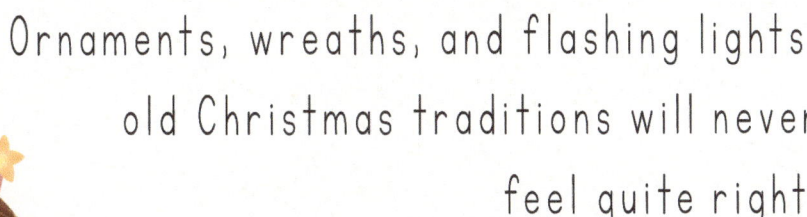

To cherish them forever,

I'll make something new.

Create a

SPECIAL STOCKING

is just what I'll do!

Christmas

🎁

Homemade Gifts

HOW-TO MAKE

🧦

Stockings

SEWING

FOR BEGINNERS

WOODWORK

KNITTING

FLOWER PAINTING

ACRYLICS

CRAFTS 4 KIDS

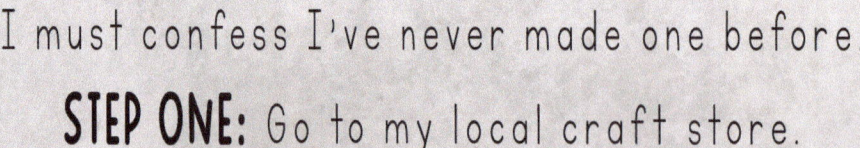

I must confess I've never made one before.

STEP ONE: Go to my local craft store.

EMBROIDERY

CROCHET

WATERCOLORS

CRAFT A DAY

BEADS

Craft Store

PERFECT! WHAT FUN! I see everything and more.
I have found exactly what I was looking for.

STEP TWO: Lay out fabric and trace a stocking shape.

CUT, THEN STITCH!

This feels like a calm and soothing escape.

STEP THREE: Add glitter!
Sparkle! A bit of pizzazz!

Iron-on snowflakes for
that razzmatazz.

Fuzzy pom-poms, jingle bells galore.

I'll write their name, so we know who it's for.

The stocking is done

and beautifully displayed.

I'M REALLY PROUD

of this creation I have made.

On top of the mantle is

where it will stay,

soaking in

PEACE AND LOVE

everyday.

It's still, and quiet, and

I love that it's there.

It shows I miss them and

will always care.

Fill the stocking, if that's right for you.
Christmas cards or trinkets, whatever
you choose to do.

A HAT,

OR A BEAR,

OR A DRAWING OF US THREE.

But these don't feel quite
right for me.

Perhaps a **POEM.**

I'm not sure what to say.

For now, I'll

TAKE A BREAK

and decide later on today.

I have fantastic ideas.
I'm glad to report.
Dessert can also be a

YUMMY

form of support.

In the kitchen, I bake,

BAKE, BAKE, BAKE!

Sugar cookies, gingerbread,

and a loaf of Ellie's fruit cake.

FORGET ALL THAT BAKING, it's snowing outside!

I'll build a snowman while Ellie tries to hide.

Tomorrow is **CHRISTMAS.**
Their gift is not complete.
I'll take time to think while
we stroll down our street.

My neighborhood
is filled with
TWINKLING LIGHTS.
Nothing is better than
being out here at night.

I've figured it out! I know what to write.
I can read this letter each
and every night.

Dearest loved one,

I miss you to the moon.
Send a sign that you're here with us,
and make it very soon!

Maybe a perched bird of red,
or squirrels dancing in the trees.
The sweet smell of candy canes.
I can find some peace in these.

I hope you know we love you so,
no matter how many years go by.
We will hug each other tight,
and remember you tonight,
alway looking up to your bright night sky.

Love, Eden & Ellie xox

THIS CHRISTMAS IS NOT LIKE BEFORE.
Still, they're with us in a way,
and they truly wish us the most magical time
on this Christmas day.

PAPER MEMORIAL STOCKING

(Always ask a grown up first)

Materials Needed:

· 2 sheets of large construction paper
· Safety scissors
· Long piece of yarn (or ribbon)
· Tape
· Crayons and/or markers
· Hole Punch
· Bonus decoration items: stickers, stick-on gems, paint, etc.

1.) Trace a large stocking shape on construction paper, then place a second piece of paper underneath.

2.) Cut out your stocking. (You should have two now!)

3.) Stack the stockings together and hole punch the edges (except for the very top for our opening).

4.) Optional: Tape the ends of your yarn (for easier "sewing", think shoelace tips).

5.) Tie your yarn to the first hole on either side.

6.) Now, lace in and out with your yarn until you reach the end. Then tie again and cut any excess yarn.

7.) Finally, color and decorate your stocking!

8.) If you'd like, you can add your loved one's name at the top. Then, fill the stocking with a letter, Christmas card, or special things to remember them by.

Place a sweet picture here

Dear _____

_____

_____

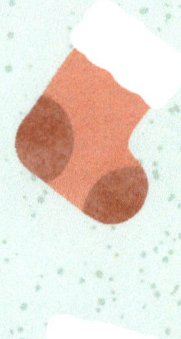

_____

_____

_____

_____

_____

_____

_____

_____

_____

_____

_____

Dear Caregivers,

The holiday season can be filled with so many expectations for a joyous celebration. The weather, smells, decorations, gifts, and traditions can collectively create an all-consuming sensory experience that floods the system. But during the holidays, it becomes even more obvious what (or who) is missing from the celebration. It becomes a time when grief colors every experience.

Like adults, kids have a large range of grief-related emotions that surface during the holiday season. They may feel sadness, anger, and an immense amount of longing for their person. They can even experience a sense of connection, joy, love, and peace. Often, these emotions can swing between the extremes or even occur concurrently. This can be confusing for children, so validating the mix of emotions that they [and you] are feeling is helpful.

Each child will have their own unique needs while experiencing grief through the holiday season. Some children may feel supported by being given some options on how to connect and remember their person who died. Other children may want to refocus their attention by engaging in activities that bring them joy or bring them away from prior traditions that may be too painful to currently experience.

It is important to validate that children can feel both happy and sad during the holiday season. Some children may feel guilty for being excited about the holidays. It is OKAY to feel it all.

How can we create space for connection and healing for children through the holidays? It is all about meeting children where they are in the moment, validating emotions that come up, and creating space to actively do something with their grief.

Here are some ideas that may feel right for your grieving child(ren):

Decorate a memory box, create a stocking or ornament, light a candle, make a favorite holiday recipe, get an item 'for' the person who died (eg. something decorative or a piece of clothing that reminds you of them), have an item 'from' them as a gift (an item that would remind you of them), acts of kindness in honor of them, include their name or something symbolic of them on holiday cards or pictures, play their favorite holiday music, have their picture out with decorations, read books that make you think of them or connects with your grief experience, take a walk in nature, donate to charity, or purely just ask them what they would like to do this year. Decide together which traditions you want to keep and which you would like to pass on this year. Kids can be the best teachers-we just need to listen.

Whatever you and your family decide to do to help your aching hearts this holiday season is the right choice for you. There are many resources and support options to help you navigate this difficult season and the vevolution of the grief journey.

You are not alone. Sending lots of love and hugs your way.

Jessica Correnti, MS, CCLS
Certified Child Life Specialist
Owner and Founder of Kids Grief Support
www.kidsgriefsupport.com

www.ingramcontent.com/pod-product-compliance
Lightning Source LLC
Chambersburg PA
CBHW041619120626
46551CB00003B/500